CONSTRUCTION LIENS FOR THE
PACIFIC NORTHWEST ALASKA
IDAHO OREGON WASHINGTON
FEDERAL PUBLIC WORKS

CONSTRUCTION LIENS FOR THE PACIFIC NORTHWEST ALASKA IDAHO OREGON WASHINGTON FEDERAL PUBLIC WORKS

A PRIMER

James H. Hopkins JD

iUniverse, Inc.
Bloomington

CONSTRUCTION LIENS FOR THE PACIFIC NORTHWEST ALASKA IDAHO OREGON WASHINGTON FEDERAL PUBLIC WORKS
A PRIMER

iUniverse books may be ordered through booksellers or by contacting:

iUniverse
1663 Liberty Drive
Bloomington, IN 47403
www.iuniverse.com
1-800-Authors (1-800-288-4677)

ISBN: 978-1-4620-3085-9 (pbk)
ISBN: 978-1-4620-3086-6 (ebk)

Printed in the United States of America

iUniverse rev. date: 07/01/2011

CONTENTS

LIEN AND CLAIM OUTLINE AND PROCEDURES PRIVATE AND PUBLIC FOR WASHINGTON

BOND CLAIM OUTLINE AND PROCEDURES FEDERAL PUBLIC WORKS

FORWARD

The material in this primer on liens for public and private construction projects in Alaska, Idaho, Oregon and Washington along with Federal Projects has been compiled for the purpose of assisting businesses and individuals in protecting their lien rights. Many helpful suggestions are included. This manual is not intended to take the place of competent legal counsel, but merely to serve as a basic guide to those who care to refer to its content.

Some statements are legally imprecise to provide practical assistance and to avoid being overly technical. Where there are ambiguities or several choices, the author has attempted to set out an approach which protects the reader and keeps the outline as simple as possible.

This manual should not be considered a legal authority, and any questions arising out of its content should be referred to counsel.

ACKNOWLEDGMENT

This volume is dedicated to the professionals who work in the construction industry

James H. Hopkins JD SPHR.

LIEN AND CLAIM OUTLINE
AND PROCEDURES
PRIVATE AND PUBLIC
FOR
ALASKA

INDEX TO
ALASKA'S MECHANICS AND
MATERIALMEN'S STATUTE
(AS 34.35.050 et seq.)

FORMS

LIEN SUMMARY
NOTICE OF RIGHT TO LIEN
NOTICE OF NON-RESPONSIBILITY
NOTICE OF COMPLETION
NOTICE TO CLAIMANT OF THE RECORDING OF A NOTICE
OF COMPLETION
NOTICE OF CLAIM OF LIEN OF LABORER OR
MATERIALMEN

ALASKA'S MECHANICS AND MATERIALMEN'S STATUTE
(AS 34.35.050 et seq.)

SEE FORM A

I. GENERAL INFORMATION

    A. Who has a construction lien? (AS 34.35.050)
        1. Generally. Any contractor, laborer, supplier, engineer, surveyor or other professional services or equipment provider or trustee of an employee benefit plan.
        2. Activities creating lien
           a) The construction, alteration, or repair of a building or improvement.
           b) The furnishing and delivering materials and/or equipment to real property under a contract with the owner or the agent of the owner which are incorporated in the construction, alteration, or repair of a building or improvement
           c) Preparing architectural or engineering plans or drawings, for the construction, alteration or repair, whether or not actually implemented.
           d) General contracting.
    B. What is covered by the lien? (AS 34.35.055)
        1. The land where the services, materials and/or equipment is used.

2. Professional services need not result in actual implementation to create lien. The professional services must be specifically requested for a partial of real property.

C. <u>Who has authority to order work-giving rise to a lien? (AS 34.35.050)</u>

1. <u>Generally</u>: the work or materials must be furnished at the request of the owner having an interest in the property or by the owner's agent to be lienable.

2. <u>Agent of Owner (AS 34.35.115)</u>: the owner's agents for purposes of creating a lien are:

   a) A Contractor,
   b) Subcontractor,
   c) Architect,
   d) Builder, or
   e) Anyone in charge of the construction project

II.   REQUIREMENT PRIOR TO CLAIMING A LIEN

A. Notice of right to lien (AS 34.35.064)
1. Prior to first delivery, provider of labor, material, services or equipment may provide a notice to the owner or the owner's agent, of the claimant's right to file a lien.
2. When this notice is given, the burden of proof regarding owner's knowledge of consent to the furnishing of labor, materials, services or equipment shifts to the owner.

SEE FORM B

3. When requested by an owner, lender or contractor, a claimant must provide amount owed. The information must be provided within five (5) days of the request. Notice of right to claim a lien may be recorded.
B. Notice of non-responsibility (AS 34.35.065)
1. An owner can defeat a lienable interest if:
    a) Within three (3) days of becoming aware of construction, he/she post a notice on the real property that he/she will not be responsible for construction alteration or repairs completed on the property;
    b) Notice is conspicuously posted;
    c) Notice is signed by two attesting witnesses or notary;
    d) Posting is witnessed;
    e) Copy is recorded

III.   CLAIMING A LIEN

   A. Notice of completion (AS 34.35.071)
       1. An owner may announce the date of completion of a project.
       2. Provide notice to all that provide notice of right to claim a lien five (5) days prior to recording the notice of completion.
       3. Provide notice of completion to any lenders ten—(10) days before recording notice of completion.
       4. Records notice of completion in district where real property is located.
       5. A notice of completion is not effective if filed before completion of the project.

SEE FORM D

   B. Claim of lien (AS 34.35.070)
       1. A claim of lien may be recorded anytime after entering into a contract for a construction project.

SEE FORM F

       2. In the event a notice of completion is not recorded, a claim of lien may not be recorded later than 90 days after a claimant:
           a. Completes a construction project;
           b. Ceases to furnish labor, materials, services or equipment.

3. In the event a notice of completion is recorded, a claim of lien may not be recorded later than 15 days after the notice of completion is recorded if the claimant (AS 34.35.068):
   a. Has advanced notice of recording the notice of completion.

SEE FORM E

   b. Has not given a notice to right to claim a lien.

SEE FORM B

C. Bond (AS 34.35.072)
   1. An owner, a prime contractor or a subcontractor who disputes the validity of a claim of lien may record a bond in the principal amount of 11/2 times the amount of the lien.
   2. The claim of lien then attaches to the bond and releases the property.

IV. DURATION OF LIEN (AS 34.35.080)

A. A recorded lien is valid for a six months from the date of recording, unless:
   1. An enforcement action is commenced in court within that time frame or;
   2. An extension for an additional six-month period is recorded.
   3. An enforcement action must then be commenced with the period of the extension.

V. ACTION TO ENFORCE A LIEN (AS 34.35.110)

A. Must be brought in Superior Court
B. Reasonable attorney's fees and cost of filing and recording the lien are recoverable.

VI. PRIORITIES AS TO VARIOUS LIEN CLAIMANTS (AS 34.35.112)

A. Lien priorities
   If more than one lien created under the Lien Statute is claimed against the property, the rank of each lien or class of liens will be in the following order:
   1. Liens of all persons other than prime contractors or subcontractors with lien rights.
   2. Liens of Trustees of any employment benefit trusts.
   3. Liens of all materialmen and subcontractors.
   4. Liens for plan preparation, surveys, architectural or engineering work, prime contractors other than the General Contractor on the project.
   5. Liens of the General Contractor.
B. If the proceeds of the foreclosure sale of the property are insufficient to pay the lien claims of all persons who have recorded claims of liens, the lien will be paid as follows:
   1. Those liens of all persons other than prime contractors or subcontractors with lien rights, shall first be paid in full, or pro rata if the proceeds are insufficient to pay them in full;

2. Those liens of trustees of employment benefit trusts shall be paid in full or pro rata if the proceeds are insufficient to pay them in full;
3. Those liens of materialmen and subcontractors shall be paid in full or pro rata if the proceeds are insufficient to pay them in full;
4. Those liens for plan preparation, surveys, architectural or engineering work, prime contractors other than the General Contractor on the project shall be paid in full or pro rata if the remainder is insufficient to pay them in full; and
5. Lien of the General Contractor shall be paid out of the balance.

C. If the proceeds of the foreclosure sale of the property are sufficient to pay the lien claims of all persons who have recorded claims of lien, the balance shall be paid to the person who owned the property before the foreclosure sale.

LIEN SUMMARY

Type: Alaska   Job No._____
             Private Work   P.O. No. _____

Owner's Residence or Place of Business	Jobsite	General Contractor or Agent	Architect

☐   Preliminary Notice   Send Notice of Right to Lien (Form B) to the owner by registered or certified mail return receipt requested, before first delivery. Also, send copy to the General Contractor or Agent.

A) Preliminary Notice_____ Date Nos._____
B) First Delivery Date_____
C) First Invoice No._____

☐   Final Notice   Record Lien Notice
     and Lien   (FormF)nolaterthan90
                          days after last delivery
                          or performance with
                          District   Recorder
                          where project is located
                          (or request attorney to
                          do so)

A) Last Delivery Date or Performance Date_____

B) Final Notice and Lien Date No._____ Nos. _____

C) Legal Description Secured_____

D) Last Invoice No._____

E) District Recorders Date District_____

☐   Start Suit   Notify attorney to
                          start suit within 6
                          months after lien filed,
                          or renew the lien for
                          additional 6 months.
                          Allow sufficient time
                          for attorney to prepare
                          suit (recommend no
                          later than 90 days
                          prior to expiration of 6
                          months).

A) Notification of Attorney Date _____
B) Send Copies to Attorney
  1) Lien Summary
  2) Contract and Invoices
  3) Payment Ledger Schedule
  4) Preliminary Notice and evidence of mailing and receipt
  5) Final Notice and Lien with evidence of mailing
  6) Additional Charges
  7) Legal Description of Property

FORM A

NOTICE OF RIGHT TO LIEN

To: (owner or agent of owner)

You are notified that
_____ (claimant)
_____

whose address is

_____

asserts a right to lien and may be entitled to record a claim of lien against the following real property:

(legal description of property)
_____

_____

The real property is owned by

The lien is claimed in respect of labor/materials/services/ equipment of the following general description, furnished or to be furnished in connection with a project on the above property:

_____

Such labor/materials/services/equipment have been or are to be provided by claimant under a contract with

(name of person with whom claimant contracted)
_____

whose address is

_____

WARNING: Unless provision is made for payment of sums that may be due to the undersigned, your above property may be subject to foreclosure to satisfy those sums even though you may pay a prime contractor or other person for the labor, material, service, or equipment furnished by the undersigned.

Dated at_____ on_____ , 20____ .

(signature of claimant)_____

(claimant's address)_____

cc: claimant's customer

FORM B

NOTICE OF NON-RESPONSIBILITY

_____(name of owner)_____ of ____(address)_____,
The owner [or if not owner of full legal title, describe the
nature of the interest held in the property] of _____(legal
description of property)_____
gives notice that any construction, alteration or repair
performed on the above property is not being furnished at
his/her/its instance. The above owner is not and will not be
responsible for any labor, material, services or equipment
provided or to be provided in connection with any such
construction, alteration or repair on the property.

This notice was posted on the property on _____(d a t e)_
in the presence of the witness whose signature appears
below, and it will be recorded in (recording office) within 3
days of posting.

   (date)_____   _____(signature)_____
                    Owner/holder of interest in
                    property

I attest that this notice was posted in my presence

_____(Witness)

We attest that this notice was signed in our presence

1._____
(Witnesses)

2._____

FORM C

NOTICE OF COMPLETION

The undersigned _____ (owner's name)____
of ____(owner's address)_____ , the owner of/holder
of an interest in real property described as _____(l e g a l
description of property sufficient for identification)____
situated in ___(recording district)___ announces that the
project relating to the construction/alteration/repair
of ____(describe the improvement)_____ upon the above
property was completed on _____(date of completion)_.

The nature of the owner's interest in estate in the
property is_____

The general contractor for the project is _____

All persons claiming mechanics' liens on the property are
notified to file their claims of lien or notices of right to lien
as required by AS 34.35.068.

Dated_____ , 20____ .

_____(signature)_____
(Owner)

State of Alaska,_____ Judicial district ss.

I_____ being first duly
sworn, depose and say that:

I am the owner of [holder of interest in] the property described in the above notice. I have read the above notice. I have knowledge of the facts stated therein, and I believe those facts to be true and correct, to the best of my knowledge, information and belief.

_____(signature)_____

Subscribed and sworn to before me this_____
day of _____, 20____.

_____
Notary Public for Alaska
My commission expires_____

FORM D

NOTICE TO CLAIMANT OF THE RECORDING OF A NOTICE OF COMPLETION

To: _____ (claimant's name) _____
_____ (address) _____

Please take notice that the Notice of Completion, a copy of which is attached, will be recorded after 5 days have elapsed from the date* of this notice.

The Notice of Completion will be recorded in (recording office for district in which property is situated), State of Alaska.

Dated_____, 20___.

_____
Owner

_____
Address

[Copy of Notice of Completion attached (FORM D)]

FORM E

_____)	
_____)	
Claimant,)	**NOTICE OF CLAIM OF LIEN OF**
)	**LABORER OR MATERIALMEN**
_____)	
Owner.)	
)	

NOTICE IS HEREBY GIVEN that on the ___ day of _____, 20_, at the request of _____, whose address is _____, the above-named claimant, whose address is _____ _____, commenced to perform labor or furnish materials or supply equipment for that certain building consisting of a _____, situated upon the following described real property, to-wit:
 of which property _____ was and is the owner; the performance of which labor or furnishing of which materials ceased on the day of , 20_, and that ninety (90) days have not elapsed since that date.
The following is a general description of the labor, materials or equipment furnished: _____ _____. The contract price for this labor, materials or equipment is $_____, and for which labor, materials, or herein described and the buildings situated thereon for the amount due said claimant, to-wit: $_____.

FORM F

[Claimant]

By:_____

STATE OF_____)
_____) ss.
JUDICIAL DISTRICT/COUNTY OF_____)

_____, being sworn,
says: I am the _____ of/for the
above-named claimant; I have knowledge of the facts; I
have read the foregoing claim, know the contents thereof,
and believe the same to be true.

_____

SIGNED AND SWORN to before me on _____, 20___.

_____
NOTARY PUBLIC in and for the State of
_____, residing at_____
_____
My Commission expires:_____

INDEX TO
BOND CLAIMS ALASKA
PUBLIC WORKS
(AS 36.25.010 et seq.)

ALASKA

PUBLIC WORKS
BOND CLAIMS
(AS 36.25.010 et seq.)
SEE FORM A

I.   <u>WHEN A BOND IS REQUIRED (AS 36.25.010)</u>

   A. On contracts in excess of $100,000 for construction, alteration or repair of any public building or public works of the state or political subdivision.

   B. The amount of the bond required is:
      1. Fifty percent of the contract amount when the contract price is less than $1,000,000
      2. Forty percent of the contract amount when the contract amount is in excess of $1,000,000, but less than $5,000,000; and
      3. $2,500,000 when the amount of the contract is in excess of $5,000,000

II.   <u>PARTIES PROTECTED BY THE BOND (AS 36.25.020)</u>

   A. Any person or firm involved in public works, as described previously, who:
      1. Has a direct contractual relationship with the contractor; or
      2. Has a direct contractual relationship with a subcontractor

III. NOTICE REQUIREMENTS (AS 36.25.020)

    A. Anyone not having a contractual relationship with the contractor must give a notice to the contractor within <u>90 days</u> of the last day of furnishing labor or materials.

    B. Notice must be provided via registered mail to the contractor.

    C. The notice must provide with substantial accuracy:

        1. The amount claimed;

        2. The name of the party who was furnished the labor or material.

SEE FORM B

IV. FORECLOSURE OF CLAIM AGAINST BOND (AS 36.25.020(c))

    A. A foreclosure action must be commenced within one year after "final settlement of the contract."

V. PRIORITY OF CLAIMS

    A. The statute does not establish any priority for payment of claims. Based on this, when the total claims against the bond exceed the amount of the bond, the claims would probably be paid on a pro rata basis.

CLAIM SUMMARY

Office Procedure Form

Type: Alaska   Job No.

               Public   Work P.O. No.

Public Body Address	Jobsite	General Contractor or Agent	Architect

☐ Preliminary   No Preliminary Notice
     Notice   necessary.

A) First Delivery Date _____
B) Preliminary Notice Date: <u>None</u>   Nos. <u>None</u>
C) First Invoice No. _____

☐ Notice of Claim   Notice of Claim Send Notice of Claim (Form B) by registered mail, return receipt requested, within 1-90 days after last delivery or performance to the General Contractor or Agent with copies to the Bonding Company and public body.

A) Last Delivery Date or Performance Date _____

B) Notice of Claim Date _____ No. _____

C) First Invoice No. _____

D) Last Invoice No. _____

E) Bonding Co. Name_____ Address _____

District _____

☐ Commence Foreclosure Action   Notify attorney to commence foreclosure action within one year after last delivery or performance.

A) Notification of Attorney Date _____
B) Send Copies to Attorney
    1) Claim Summary
    2) Contract and Invoices
    3) Payment Ledger Schedule
    4) Preliminary Notice and evidence of mailing and receipt
    5) Notice of Claim with evidence of mailing
    6) District Marshal Record—Not Necessary
    7) Additional Charges

FORM A

NOTICE TO CONTRACTOR

TO: _____(prime contractor)_____

You are hereby notified that the undersigned claimant has furnished (labor, materials, supplies or equipment) for use in the prosecution of the work of (public agency, contract number) at the request of (name of subcontractor). The last day of furnishing (labor, materials, supplies or equipment)_____was. The undersigned makes claim against you and your surety for payment of $_____which sum is due and owing to the undersigned.

DATED this _____day of , 20____.

Name of Claimant _____
Address _____
Phone _____
Number _____

_____
Signature
Title _____
Contractor Registration Number _____

LIEN AND CLAIM OUTLINE AND PROCEDURES PRIVATE AND PUBLIC FOR IDAHO

INDEX TO
IDAHO MECHANIC'S AND MATERIALMEN'S STATUTE
(IC 45-501, et seq.)

FORMS

IDAHO MECHANIC'S AND MATERIALMEN'S STATUTE

IC 45-501, et seq.

SEE FORM A

I.   GENERAL INFORMATION

A. WHO HAS A CONSTRUCTION LIEN? (IC 45-501)
    1. Generally: Anyone that provides labor, materials; architect, engineer or surveyor who furnishes labor or professional services.
        b) Providing materials includes renting or leasing equipment, supplies and/or fixtures.
    2. Activities Creating Liens
        a) Building and Structures: The construction, alteration or repair of any building or structure.
        b) Clearing, Grading and Filling: Anyone doing grading, leveling, filling and/or surfacing on any land.
        c) Professional Services: Anyone surveying, establishing or marking the boundaries of, preparing maps, plans, or specifications for estimates of cost, on site observation or supervision, or inspecting, testing or otherwise performing any other

architectural or engineering services for the improvement of real property.

B. <u>LIEN FOR IMPROVING LOTS (IC 45-504)</u>

1. Any person who, at the request of the owner of any lot in any incorporated city or town, surveys, grades, fills in, or otherwise improves the lot, or the street in front of or adjoining the lot, has a lien upon such lot for his work done or material furnished.

C. <u>WHAT IS SUBJECT TO THE LIEN: (IC 45-505)</u> The land upon which or in connection with which any professional services are performed or any building, improvement or structure that is built, along with the convenient space around it, may be subject to the lien, if, at the commencement of the furnishing of professional services or material or other work, the owner ordered the professional services or improvement or structure to be built, altered or repaired., When someone owns less than fee simple in the land, then only the interest owned is subject to such lien.

D. WHO HAS THE AUTHORITY TO ORDER WORK GIVING RISE TO A LIEN? (IC 45-501)

1. <u>Generally:</u> The work or materials must be furnished at the request of the owner of the property, or by the owner's agent.

2. <u>Agent:</u>
   a) Is any Contractor, subcontractor, architect, builder or any person having charge of the construction or other improvements.

II.   FILING THE LIEN

A. CREATING THE LIEN (IC 45-507)
1. <u>Lien Filing Requirements</u>: The Claim of Lien must be recorded with the county recorder in the county where the property is located, within 90 days from completion of the labor, furnishing the materials, or services. The Lien must be served or mailed by certified or registered mail to the owner <u>within five (5) business days of recording</u>.
2. <u>Contents of Claim of Lien</u>
    a. The name, the address and phone number of the claimant;
    b. The name of the person who has the contract with the claimant;
    c. The name of the owner or the person reputed to be the owner of the property. If the owner is not known, state not known.
    d. The description of the property reasonably sufficient for identification. If at all possible, the property should be described by a complete legal description.
    e. The principal amount claimed.
    f. The claim must be verified by oath, as to its accuracy, by the claimant, claimant's agent or attorney.

SEE FORM B

B. THE AMOUNT OF THE LIEN (IC 45-507)
1. <u>Generally</u>: The lien is for the unpaid amount after credits and offsets.

2. Costs and Attorney Fees (IC 45-513): Any number of persons claiming a lien in the same property may join in the same action. The court shall allow filing and recording costs and reasonable attorneys' fees.

III. FORECLOSING THE LIEN

A. LAWSUIT MUST BE FILED WITHIN SIX MONTHS (IC 45-510)
   Once a Claim of Lien has been filed, legal action to enforce the lien must be commenced within six months, or the lien expires.
B. BOND IN LIEU OF LIEN (IC 45-519)
   1. Generally: The debtor of the claimant or a party in interest (petitioner) may petition for a surety bond with the lien claimant as principal. Then, the lien releases from the land and attaches only to the bond.

SEE FORM C

C. PETITION FOR BOND IN LIEU OF LIEN (IC 45-520)
   1. The petitioner shall obtain an order from the district court of the county where the property is located, setting forth the date and time for a hearing on the petition.
      The time and date of the hearing must be set at least five (5) days after the date of the order, but not more than ten (10) days.
   2. A copy of the petition and the order must be served on the lien claimant not less than two

(2) days before the date of the hearing in the same manner as a summons.

SEE FORM D

IV. PRIORITY IN FORECLOSURE ACTION (IC 45-512)

A. WHO HAS PRIORITY IN A FORECLOSURE ACTION?
 1. All laborers, other than contractors or subcontractors
 2. All materialmen, other than contractors or subcontractors
 3. The original contractor
 4. All professional engineers and licensed surveyors

B. APPLICATION OF PROCEEDS FROM SALE OF PROPERTY IN A LIEN FORECLOSURE
 1. The proceeds from the sale of any property sold in a lien foreclosure action is applied first to pay liens in a class before any is applied to pay the next lower class. When there are not enough proceeds to pay an entire class in full, then the proceeds are applied pro rata to that class.

LIEN SUMMARY

Office Procedure Form

Type: Idaho   Job No.
                 Private Work   P.O. No.

Owner's Residence or Place of Business	Jobsite	General Contractor or Agent	Architect

A) First Delivery Date or Commencement of Services _____

B) First Invoice No. _____and due date _____

☐ Lien Claim   Record Lien Claim (Form B) within 90 days after last delivery or performance with County Recorder where project is located. Send copy to Owner within 24 hours of recording.

A) Last Delivery Date or Performance Date _____

B) Lien Date _____No._____

C) Legal Description Secured _____

D) Last Invoice No. _____
E) County Recorder Recording _____Date County _____

___

☐ Commence Foreclosure Action

Notify attorney to commence foreclosure action within six (6) months after recording final notice with County Recorder. Allow sufficient time for attorney to prepare foreclosure action (recommended no later than 90 days prior to expiration of six (6) months).

A) Notification of Attorney Date _____
B) Send Copies to Attorney
  1) Lien Summary
  2) Contract and Invoices
  3) Payment Ledger Schedule
  4) Preliminary Notice and evidence of mailing and receipt
  5) Final Notice and Lien with evidence of mailing
  6) Additional Charges
  7) Legal Description of Property

FORM A

After recording return to:

_____[claimant]

_____[address]

CLAIM OF LIEN

_____, Claimant vs. (name of person indebted to claimant)_____

Notice is hereby given that the person named below claims a lien pursuant to chapter 60.04 RCW. In support of this lien the following information is submitted:

1. NAME OF LIEN CLAIMANT: _____
   TELEPHONE NUMBER: _____
   ADDRESS: _____

2. DATE ON WHICH THE CLAIMANT BEGAN TO PERFORM LABOR, PROVIDE PROFESSIONAL SERVICES, SUPPLY MATERIAL OR EQUIPMENT OR DATE ON WHICH EMPLOYEE BENEFIT CONTRIBUTIONS BECAME DUE:

   _____

3. NAME OF PERSON INDEBTED TO THE CLAIMANT:

4. DESCRIPTION OF THE PROPERTY AGAINST WHICH A LIEN IS CLAIMED (street address, legal description or other information that will reasonably describe the property):

_____

_____

_____

5. NAME OF THE OWNER OR REPUTED OWNER (If not known state "unknown"):

_____

6. THE LAST DATE ON WHICH LABOR WAS PERFORMED; PROFESSIONAL SERVICES WERE FURNISHED; CONTRIBUTIONS TO AN EMPLOYEE BENEFIT PLAN WERE DUE: OR MATERIAL, OR EQUIPMENT WAS FURNISHED:

_____

7. PRINCIPAL AMOUNT FOR WHICH THE LIEN IS CLAIMED:

_____

8. IF THE CLAIMANT IS THE ASSIGNEE OF THIS CLAIM SO STATE HERE:

_____

                          _____

                          Claimant

                          _____

                          [address]

FORM B

STATE OF IDAHO   )
) ss.
COUNTY OF _____)

I, _____, being sworn, says:

I am the claimant above-named; I have read or heard the foregoing Claim of Lien, read and know the contents thereof, and believe the same to be true and correct.

Claimant_____

GIVEN UNDER MY HAND AND OFFICIAL SEAL this ____
_____ day of _____, 20___ .

_____
NOTARY PUBLIC in and for the
State of Idaho, residing at
My Commission Expires:

FORM B-2

BOND FOR RELEASE OF LIEN
[TITLE OF COURT IF ACTION HAS COMMENCED]

In re the matter of the petition of:	NO:
_____	PETITION FOR RELEASE OF MECHANIC'S LIEN OF UPON POSTING OF SURETY BOND

WHEREAS, _____*[name of owner, contractor, or other person disputing the lien]*___desires to give a bond for releasing the following described real property from that certain claim of mechanic's lien in the sum of $____ _____, recorded _____, in the office of the recorder in __*[name of county where the real property is situated]*:

NOW, THEREFORE, the undersigned principal and surety do hereby obligate themselves to __*[name of claimant]*__, the claimant named in the mechanic's lien, under the conditions prescribed by sections 45-518 through 45-524, Idaho Code, inclusive, in the sum of $ *[1-1/2 x claim]*, from which sum they will pay the claimant such amount as a court of competent jurisdiction may adjudge to have been secured by his lien, with interest, costs, and attorney's fees.

IN WITNESS WHEREOF, the principal and surety have executed this bond at _____, Idaho, on the day of _____.

_____

[Signature of Principal]
SURETY COMPANY

By: *[Its Attorney-in-Fact]*__

FORM C

STATE OF IDAHO   )
) ss:
COUNTY OF   )

    On _____, before me, the undersigned, a notary public of this county and state, personally appeared _____ who acknowledged that he executed the foregoing instrument as principal for the purposes therein mentioned and also personally appeared _____ _____known (or satisfactorily proved) to me to be the attorney in fact of the corporation that executed the foregoing instrument, and known to me to be the person who executed that instrument on behalf of the corporation named therein, and he acknowledged to me that that corporation executed the foregoing instrument.

                        _____

                        NOTARY PUBLIC in and for the State of Idaho, residing at _____
My Commission expires: _____

FORM C-2

PETITION FOR RELEASE OF LIEN
BY POSTING BOND

(a) The title of the cause, thus: "In the matter of the petition of _____(name of petitioner) for release of mechanic's lien of _____ _____(name of mechanic's lien claimant) upon posting surety bond."

(b) An allegation of the purchase of and payment of the premium for the bond, and the dates of purchase and payment.

(c) An allegation incorporating by reference a true copy of the bond, which copy must be attached to the petition.

(d) The name and names of the owner or reputed owners of the land subject to the lien.

(e) A description of the real property subject to the lien, and the instrument number of the lien as given by the recorder's office.

(f) A prayer for an order releasing the lien.

FORM D

_____

Claimant

_____

Defendant

    KNOW ALL PERSONS BY THESE PRESENTS, that a certain Lien, claimed by Lien Notice filed and recorded in the office of the County Recorder of _____ County, Idaho, on the _____ day of _____, 20____, recorded under Recording No. _____ , by the above-named claimant against the above-named defendant, for the sum of _____ Dollars ($____) upon the following property:

_____

_____

_____

is paid and satisfied, and the same is hereby released.

_____

Claimant

_____

[address]

FORM E

STATE OF IDAHO   )
) ss.
COUNTY OF   )

I, _____, being sworn, says:

I am the claimant above-named; I have read or heard the foregoing Release of Lien, read and know the contents thereof, and believe the same to be true and correct.

_____
Claimant

GIVEN UNDER MY HAND AND OFFICIAL SEAL this day of _____, 20_____.

_____
NOTARY PUBLIC in and for the State of Idaho, residing at _____
My Commission Expires: _____

FORM E-2

_____

Claimant

PARTIAL RELEASE OF LIEN

_____

Defendant

KNOW ALL PERSONS BY THESE PRESENTS, that a certain Lien, claimed by Lien Notice filed and recorded in the office of the County Recorder of _____ _____ County, Idaho, on the day of _____ _____, 20___, recorded under Recording No. , by the above-named claimant against the above-named defendant, for the sum of _____Dollars ($_____) upon the following property:

has been partially paid and is partially satisfied in the amount of $ _____, and the same is hereby partially released in said amount.

_____

Claimant

_____

_____

[address]

50

FORM F

STATE OF IDAHO   )
) ss.
COUNTY OF   )

I,_____, being sworn, says:

I am the claimant above-named; I have read or heard the foregoing Release of Lien, read and know the contents thereof, and believe the same to be true and correct.

_____

Claimant

GIVEN UNDER MY HAND AND OFFICIAL SEAL this day _____of , 20_____.

_____

NOTARY PUBLIC in and for the State
of Idaho, residing at _____
My Commission Expires: _____

FORM F-2

_____

Claimant

CONDITIONAL RELEASE OF LIEN

_____

Defendant

KNOW ALL PERSONS BY THESE PRESENTS, that a certain Lien, claimed by Lien Notice filed and recorded in the office of _____ the County Recorder of County, Idaho, on the _____ day of _____, 20___, recorded under Recording No. _____, by the above-named claimant against the above-named defendant, for the sum of _____ _____ Dollars ($_____) upon the following property:

is hereby paid and satisfied, and the same is hereby released, conditioned upon the check in the amount of $ __ _____issued by _____clearing the bank.

_____

Claimant

_____

[address]

FORM G

STATE OF IDAHO   )
) ss.
COUNTY OF   )

I, _____, being sworn, says:

I am the claimant above-named; I have read or heard the foregoing Release of Lien, read and know the contents thereof, and believe the same to be true and correct.

_____
Claimant

GIVEN UNDER MY HAND AND OFFICIAL SEAL this day _____of, 20_____.

_____
NOTARY PUBLIC in and for the State of Idaho, residing at _____
My Commission Expires: _____

INDEX TO
BOND CLAIMS ON IDAHO PUBLIC WORKS
PROJECTS
(IC 54-1925 et seq.)

I.   WHEN A BOND IS REQUIRED (IC 54-1926)
II.   PARTIES PROTECTED BY THE BOND (IC 54-1927)
III.   NOTICE REQUIREMENTS (IC 54-1927)
IV.   FORECLOSURE OF CLAIM AGAINST BOND (IC 54-1927)

FORMS

CLAIM SUMMARY OFFICE PROCEDURE FORM
NOTICE TO CONTRACTOR

BOND CLAIMS

ON IDAHO PUBLIC WORKS PROJECTS
(IC 54-1925, et seq.)

SEE FORM A

I. WHEN A BOND IS REQUIRED (IC 54-1926)

    A. Contracts for construction, alteration or repair of any public project, require the contractor to furnish a payment bond.

    B. The amount of the bond required is fixed by the contracting body, but in no case can it be less than 85% of the contract amount.

    C. If the public body fails to obtain a bond, the public body becomes liable for the debts of those persons supplying materials and/or labor for the prosecution of work on the project (IC 54-1928).

II. PARTIES PROTECTED BY THE BOND (IC 54-1927)

    A. Persons or firms involved in work on a public construction project that have a direct contractual relationship with either:
      1. The prime contractor; or
      2. Subcontractors with a direct contractual relationship to the prime contractor.

III. **NOTICE REQUIREMENTS (IC 54-1927)**

A. Every subcontractor, supplier or laborer who does not have a direct contractual relationship with the prime contractor must give written notice to the prime contractor within 90 days of the last day of furnishing labor or materials.
B. Inspection of work already performed, nor correction of defective work extends this time period.
C. The notice must provide with substantial accuracy:
    1. The amount claimed; and
    2. The name of the subcontractor to whom the labor or material was furnished.

SEE FORM B

The notice must be provided to the contractor by registered or certified mail with return receipt requested and postage prepaid.

IV. **FORECLOSURE OF CLAIM AGAINST BOND (IC 54-1927)**

A. A foreclosure action against the bond must be commenced in state court in the county where the work took place.
B. The foreclosure action must be commenced within one year from the date of last furnishing labor or materials.
C. Attorney's fees are allowed. (IC 54-1929)

CLAIM SUMMARY

Office Procedure Form

Type: Idaho Job No.
Public Work P.O. No.

Public Body: Name and Address	Jobsite	General Contractor or Agent	Architect

☐ Preliminary Notice

No Preliminary Notice necessary.

A) First Delivery Date _____
B) First Invoice No. _____

☐ Notice of Claim   Send Notice to Contractor (Form B) by registered or certified mail, return receipt requested, no later than 90 days after last delivery or performance to the General Contractor or Agent with copies to the Bonding Company and owner.

A) Last Delivery Date or Performance Date _____

B) Final Notice and Lien Date _____No. _____

C) First Invoice No. _____

D) Last Invoice No. _____

E) Bonding Co. Name _____

Address District _____

☐ Start Suit

Notify attorney to start suit within one year after last delivery or performance.

A) Notification of Attorney Date _____

B) Send Copies to Attorney _____
    1) Lien Summary
    2) Contract and Invoices
    3) Payment Ledger Schedule
    4) Preliminary Notice—None
    5) Final Notice and Lien with evidence of mailing
    6) District Marshal Record—Not Necessary
    7) Additional Charges

FORM A

NOTICE TO CONTRACTOR

TO:_____(prime contractor)_____

You are hereby notified that the undersigned claimant has furnished (labor, materials, supplies or equipment) for use in the prosecution of the work of (public agency, contract number) at the request of (name of subcontractor). The last day of furnishing (labor, materials, supplies or equipment) was _____. The undersigned makes claim against you and your surety for payment of $ which sum is due and owing to the undersigned.

DATED this _____day of _____
_____, 20___.

Name of Claimant_____
Address _____
Phone Number _____

_____
Signature _____
Title _____
Contractor Registration Number_____

LIEN AND CLAIM OUTLINE AND PROCEDURES PRIVATE AND PUBLIC FOR OREGON

INDEX TO

OREGON MECHANIC'S AND MATERIALMEN'S STATUTE
(ORS 87.010, et seq.)

IV. OWNER'S RIGHT TO MATERIAL LIST. (OR 87.027)

V. NOTICE OF INTENT TO FORECLOSE. (OR 87.057)

VI. PRIORITY OF LIENS. (OR 87.060 (6))
    A. LIEN PRIORITIES.

FORMS

LIEN SUMMARY OFFICE PROCEDURE FORM
NOTICE OF RIGHT TO A LIEN
NOTICE OF COMPLETION

OREGON MECHANIC'S AND MATERIALMEN'S STATUTE

ORS 87.010, et seq.

SEE FORM A

I.   GENERAL INFORMATION

    A.   WHO HAS A GENERAL CONSTRUCTION LIEN? (OR 87.010)

        1.   Generally: Any person performing labor, transporting or furnishing material, renting equipment, trustees of employee benefit plans, or an architect, landscape architect, land surveyor or registered engineer.

        2.   Activities Creating a Lien

            a)   Building and Structures: The construction of any improvement.
            b)   Trustee of any Employee Benefit Plan: Contributions due an employee benefit plan due to labor performed on any improvement, required to be paid by agreement.
            c)   Professional Services: Anyone providing architectural, landscape, surveyor, or engineering services, in the preparation of plans, drawings or specifications that

are intended for the use in or to facilitate the construction of an improvement.

B. WHAT IS COVERED BY THE LIEN? (OR 87.015)

1. When used or for construction of an improvement, the lien is against the site and the improvement plus the land required for the convenient use and occupation of the improvement. When a condominium is involved the lien relates to the common elements appertaining to that unit.

C. WHO HAS THE AUTHORITY TO ORDER WORK WHICH GIVES RISE TO A LIEN? (OR 87.010)

1. Generally: The work must be at the request of the owner of the improvement, or construction agent of the owner. In the case of architect, landscape architect, land surveyor or registered agent the work must be ordered by the owner or owner's agent.

II. PERFECTION REQUIREMENTS

A. CLAIM OF LIEN

1. Notice of Right to Lien: (OR 87.021): Anyone working on residential buildings (see b. below) must give notice of right to lien within eight (8) days of first delivery of material or performance of labor, excluding Saturdays,

Sundays and Holidays. This notice will relate back and pick up all work performed the prior eight (8) days.

a) Residential Building: (OR 87.021(3)(b)(A): A residential building is a structure that will be occupied by the owner as a residence and does not contain more than four units.

b) Notice to Mortgagee (OR 87.025(3)): In order to have a priority over a recorded mortgage, the mortgagee must receive notice of right to lien within eight (8) days of first delivery of material or performance of labor, on commercial and residential properties. Giving the notice in all situations would be a good office practice.

2. Form of Notice (OR 87.023): The Statute provides for the minimum information that is required in the notice.

See Form B

3. Perfecting Lien (OR 87.035): The Claim of Lien must be recorded within 75 days after last performance of labor, delivery of material or rental of equipment, or 75 days after completion of construction, whichever is earlier.

a. Completion (OR 87.045): Completion is when the improvement is substantially complete, when a notice of completion is posted or recorded, or when the project is abandoned.

See Form C

b. Contents (OR87.045): A Claim of Lien shall contain:

1. A true statement of the net amount owed;

2. The name of the owner, or reputed owner, if known;

3. The name of the person who employed the claimant or to whom the claimant furnished the materials or rented the equipment or by whom contributions are owed; and

4. A description of the property to be liened with sufficient for identification, including the address, if known.

5. The Claim of Lien shall be verified by the oath of the person filing or of some other person having knowledge of the facts, subject to the criminal penalties for false swearing (ORS 162.075).

c. <u>Where Recorded (87.035)</u>: With the County Recorder for the county where the property is located.

d. <u>Notice of Lien Filing (OR 87.039)</u>: The notice of the Claim of Lien must be provided to the owner and to the mortgagee no later than 20 days after filing. A copy of the Claim of Lien must be attached to the Notice. Failure comply will prohibit recovery of costs and attorneys fees in any foreclosure action.

e. <u>Delivery of Notice (OR 87.018)</u>: Notice must be personally served or sent registered or certified mail.

III. <u>DURATION OF LIEN (OR 87.055)</u>

A. The lien is valid for a period of 120 days after filing.

IV. <u>OWNER'S RIGHT TO MATERIAL LIST (OR 87.027)</u>

A. The owner has the right to demand in writing a complete list of materials supplied for the project. In the event the owner so demands, the lien holder must provide such a list to the owner within fifteen (15) days, not including Saturdays, Sundays and Holidays. Failure to comply will prohibit the recovery of attorney's costs and fees in a foreclosure action.

V. NOTICE OF INTENT TO FORECLOSE (OR 87.057)

A. No later than 10 days before commencing a foreclosure action, the lien holder must give notice to the owner and mortgage holder.

B. After receipt of this notice the owner can demand a list of material and the charges or a statement and the contract bases for the money being owed. This information must be provided within 5 days.

VI. PRIORITY OF LIENS (OR 87.060 (6))

A. LIEN PRIORITIES

1. Construction lien holders have equal priority.

LIEN SUMMARY

Office Procedure Form

Type: Oregon   Job No.
              Private Work   P.O. No.

Owner's Residence or Place of Business	Jobsite	General Contractor or Agent	Architect

☐ Notice of Right to a Lien   Send <u>Notice of Right to a Lien</u> (Form B) within eight (8) days of first delivery.

A) First Delivery Date or Commencement of Services _____
B) Preliminary Notice Date _____ Nos. _____
C) First Invoice No. _____ and due date _____

☐ Final Notice and Lien

Record final notice within 75 days after last delivery or performance with County Recorder where project is located (or request attorney to do so).

A) Last Delivery Date or Performance Date _____
B) Final Notice and Lien Date _____ No. _____
C) Legal Description Secured _ _____
D) Last Invoice No. _____
E) County Recorder Recording Date_____County_____

☐ Notice of Intent to Foreclose — Ten (10) days prior to foreclosure.

☐ Commence Foreclosure Action — Notify attorney to commence foreclosure action within 120 days after recording final notice with County Recorder. Allow sufficient time for attorney to prepare foreclosure action.

FORM A

A) Notification of Attorney Date _____

B) Send Copies to Attorney

    B. 1)   Lien Summary

    C. 2)   Contract and Invoices

    D. 3)   Payment Ledger Schedule

    E. 4)   Preclaim Notice and evidence of mailing and receipt

    F. 5)   Notice of Intent

    G. 6)   Copy of Lien

    H. 7)   Additional Charges

    I. 8)   Legal Description of Property

FORM A-2

NOTICE OF RIGHT TO A LIEN
WARNING: READ THIS NOTICE

PROTECT YOURSELF FROM PAYING ANY CONTRACTOR
OR SUPPLIER TWICE FOR THE SAME SERVICE

To: Owner:_____Date of Mailing: _____

       Owner's Address: _____

This is to inform you that_____ _____
_____has begun to provide_____
_____(description of
materials, equipment, labor or services) ordered by _____
_____ for improvements to
property you own. The property is located at _____

A lien may be claimed for all materials, equipment, labor and services furnished after a date that is eight days, not including Saturdays, Sundays and other holidays as defined in ORS 187.010, before this notice was mailed to you.

Even if you or your mortgage lender have made full payment to the contractor who ordered these materials or services, your property may still be subject to a lien unless supplier providing this notice is paid.

THIS IS NOT A LIEN. It is a notice sent to you for your protection in compliance with the construction lien laws of the State of Oregon.

This notice has been sent to you by:

NAME: _____

ADDRESS: _____

TELEPHONE: _____

IF YOU HAVE ANY QUESTIONS ABOUT THIS NOTICE, FEEL FREE TO CALL US.

—IMPORTANT INFORMATION ON REVERSE SIDE—

FORM B

IMPORTANT INFORMATION
FOR YOUR PROTECTION

Under Oregon's laws, those who work on your property or provide labor, equipment, services or materials and are not paid have a right to enforce their claim for payment against your property. This claim is known as a construction lien.

If your contractor fails to pay subcontractors, material suppliers, rental equipment suppliers, service providers or laborers or neglects to make other legally required payments, the people who are owed money can look to your property for payment, even if you have paid your contractor in full.

The law states that all people hired by a contractor to provide you with materials, equipment, labor or services must give you a notice of right to lien to let you know what they have provided.

WAYS TO PROTECT
YOURSELF ARE:

• RECOGNIZE that this notice of right to lien may result in a lien against your property unless all those supplying a notice of right to a lien have been paid.

- LEARN more about the lien laws and the meaning of this notice by contacting the Construction Contractors Board, an attorney or the firm sending this notice.

- ASK for a statement of the labor, equipment, services or materials provided to your property from each party that sends you a notice of right to a lien.

- WHEN PAYING your contractor for materials, equipment, labor or services, you may make checks payable jointly to the contractor and the firm furnishing materials,

- OR use one of the methods suggested by the "Information Notice to Owners." If you have not received such a notice, contact the Construction Contractors Board.

- GET EVIDENCE that all firms from whom you have received a notice of right to a lien have been paid or have waived the right to claim a lien against your property.

- CONSULT an attorney, a professional escrow company or your mortgage lender.

FORM B-2

NOTICE OF COMPLETION

Notice hereby is given that the building, structure or other improvement on the following described premises, (insert the legal description of the property including the street address, if known) has been completed.

All persons claiming a lien upon the same under the Construction Lien Law hereby are notified to file a claim of lien as required by ORS 87.035.

Dated: _____, 20____

_____
Original Contractor, Owner or Mortgagee

Address: _____

_____

_____

INDEX TO
OREGON PUBLIC WORKS BOND CLAIMS
(ORS 279.029 & 526 et seq.)

FORMS

OREGON PUBLIC WORKS BOND CLAIMS

(ORS 279.029 & 526 et seq.)
SEE FORM A

I.   BOND

    A. BOND REQUIRED (ORS 279C.380)

       1. Any contract for a public improvement by Oregon State, or any political subdivision requires a surety bond in the amount of 100% of the contract amount, this applies only to public improvement contracts where the value, as estimated by the contracting agency, is more than $100,000 or, in the case of contracts for highways, bridges and other transportation projects, is more than $50,000.

    B. BOND NOT REQUIRED (ORS 279C.380)

       1. In case of emergency, or when the interest or property of the contracting agency or the public agency or agencies issuing the contract would suffer material injury by delay, the requirement of furnishing a payment bond may be excused.

    C. PARTIES PROTECTED (ORS 279C.600)

       1. A person supplying labor or materials for the performance of the work provided in a public contract, including any person having a direct contractual relationship with the contractor furnishing the payment bond or

a direct contractual relationship with any subcontractor.

D. NOTICE TO CONTRACTOR AND PUBLIC BODY (ORS 279C.605)

1. The person claiming against the bond must file a notice of the claim with the Contractor and the Public Body no later than 180 days after last providing labor or materials to the project.

2. The claim must be provided to:
    a) The Contractor;
    b) The Public Body;
    c) The Bonding Company; and
    d) The party with whom claimant is doing business.

3. Notice may be given by registered or certified mail return receipt or personal service and obtaining a receipt.

SEE FORM B

E. FORECLOSURE AGAINST THE SURETY BOND (ORS 279C.610)

1. The lawsuit for foreclosure of the bond is commenced in the Circuit or Federal District Court.

2. The lawsuit for foreclosure must be brought no later than 2 years after the person last provided labor or materials.

F. PRIORITY OF CLAIMS (ORS 579C.615)

1. All labor and material liens have a preference over all other liens.

G. ATTORNEY FEES (ORS 742.061)

1. A successful claimant is entitled to recover attorney fees, provided the claim is unpaid for six months after the surety was put on notice and the recovery is for more than the surety tendered on the claim.

CLAIM SUMMARY

Office Procedure Form

Type: Oregon   Job No. _____
                  Public Work   P.O. No. _____

Public Body: Name and Address	Jobsite	General Contractor or Agent	Architect

□ Preliminary Notice   Preliminary Notice is Not Required.

☐ Notice of Claim

Send Notice to Contractor and Public Body (Form B) by registered or certified mail or hand delivered no later than 120 days after the day the person last provided labor or furnished materials. The Notice may be sent or delivered to the contractor at any place the contractor maintains an office, conducts business or at the residence of the contractor.

A) Last Date Labor Provided or Materials Furnished ____

☐ Notice of Claim (Claim as a Contribution to an Employee Benefit Plan)

If the claim is for a required contribution to a fund of any employee benefit plan, notice shall be sent or delivered within 150 days after the employee last provided labor or materials.

A) Last Date Labor Provided or Materials Furnished ____

☐ Limitation on Commencement of Action	The action must be instituted no later than two years after the person last provided labor or materials.

A) Last Date Labor Provided or Materials Furnished _____

FORM A

NOTICE TO CONTRACTOR AND PUBLIC BODY

TO: (Name and address of Contractor)

TO: (Name and address of Public Body)

Notice hereby is given that the undersigned (here insert the name of the claimant) has a claim for (here insert a brief description of the labor or materials performed or furnished and the person by whom performed or furnished: if the claim is for other than labor or materials, insert a brief description of the claim) in the sum of (here insert the amount) dollars against the bond taken from (here insert the name of the principal and, if known, the surety or sureties upon the bond) for the work of (here insert a brief description of the work concerning which the bond was taken). Such material or labor was supplied to (here insert the name of the contractor or subcontractor).

DATED this _____ day of , 20____.

Name of Claimant _____

Address _____

Phone Number _____

_____

Signature

Title_____

Contractor Registration Number___

cc: Claimant's Customer   Certified mail #

Return receipt requested

Surety   Certified mail #

Return receipt requested

LIEN AND CLAIM OUTLINE AND PROCEDURES PRIVATE AND PUBLIC FOR WASHINGTON

INDEX TO

WASHINGTON MECHANIC'S AND MATERIALMEN'S STATUTE
(RCW 60.04.010, et seq.)

III. FILING THE LIEN
     A. CREATING THE LIEN (RCW 60.04.091)
         1. Lien Filing Requirements
         2. Contents of Claim of Lien
     B. RECORDING REQUIREMENT (RCW 65.04.045)
         1. County Auditor's Recorded Instrument Requirements
     C. AVAILABILITY OF INFORMATION (RCW 60.04.230 and261)
         1. Generally
     D. THE AMOUNT OF THE LIEN (RCW 60.04.091)
         1. Generally
         2. Owner-Occupied Residential Remodels

IV. FORECLOSING THE LIEN
     A. LAWSUIT MUST BE FILED WITHIN 8 MONTHS (RCW 60.04.141)
     B. BOND IN LIEU OF CLAIM (RCW 60.04.161)
         1. Generally
     C. THE "STOP PAYMENT" NOTICE TO THE LENDER (RCW 60.04.221)
         1. Generally
         2. Procedure
         3. The Effect of the Notice to the Real Property Lender
     D. THE OWNER'S RIGHTS AGAINST A LIEN CLAIMANT (RCW 60.04.81)
         1. Procedure
     E. LIEN RELEASE (RCW 60.04.071)

V. CONSUMER PROTECTION
     A. VIOLATION (RCW 60.04.035)
     B. PENALTY (RCW 19.86 et seq.)

VI. PRIORITY OF LIENS—WASHINGTON STATE
A. LIEN PRIORITIES (RCW 60.04.181)

FORMS

LIEN SUMMARY
NOTICE TO CUSTOMER
NOTICE TO OWNER
NOTICE OF FURNISHING PROFESSIONAL SERVICES
CLAIM OF LIEN
COUNTY AUDITOR INDEXING COVER SHEET
THE CONSTRUCTION SITE POSTING REQUIREMENT
NOTICE TO REAL PROPERTY LENDER
RELEASE OF LIEN
PARTIAL RELEASE OF LIEN
CONDITIONAL RELEASE OF LIEN

WASHINGTON MECHANIC'S AND MATERIALMEN'S STATUTE

RCW 60.04.011, et seq.
SEE FORM A

I. <u>GENERAL INFORMATION: The Mechanic's and Materialmen's Statute is a derogation of common law and will be strictly construed by the Courts.</u>

    A. <u>WHO HAS A CONSTRUCTION LIEN? (RCW 60.04.021)</u>

        1. <u>Generally</u>: Any contractor, laborer, supplier, architect, engineer or surveyor who furnishes labor or professional services, materials, services or equipment.

        2. <u>Activities Creating Liens</u>

            a) <u>Building and Structures</u>: The demolition, construction, alteration or repair of any building or structure.

            b) <u>Clearing, Grading and Filling</u>: Anyone doing clearing, grading and/or filling on real property. The lien may extend to off-site work on adjoining property, streets and roads.

            c) <u>Landscaping</u>: Anyone doing landscaping on real property, including the furnishing of landscaping materials.

d) <u>Professional Services</u>: Anyone surveying, establishing or marking the boundaries of, preparing maps, plans, or specifications for, or inspecting, testing, or otherwise performing any other architectural or engineering services for the improvement of real property.

e) Condominium Improvements (RCW 64.32.070): A pro-rata lien on each condominium unit.

B. <u>WHAT IS COVERED BY THE LIEN? (RCW 60.04.011)</u>

1. <u>Generally</u>: The labor performed, materials supplied, professional services or equipment furnished must actually or constructively add to or become part of the property. Professional services rendered need not result in actual construction to be lienable.

C. <u>WHO HAS THE AUTHORITY TO ORDER WORK GIVING RISE TO A LIEN? (RCW 60.04.011)</u>

1. <u>Generally</u>: The work or materials must be furnished at the request of the owner of an interest in the property, or by that party's actual or "construction agent" to be lienable.

2. <u>Construction Agent</u>

a) Licensed and registered persons: Only a licensed or registered contractor, or subcontractor, architect, engineer or person in charge of the construction is an agent of the owner.

(1) An unlicensed contractor precludes lien rights for those who deal directly with that unlicensed contractor. (RCW 60.04.041)

II.   NOTICE REQUIREMENTS PRIOR TO FILING A LIEN

   A.   NOTICE TO CUSTOMER (RCW 18.27.114)
   A contractor who contracts directly with an owner (including tenants) on: (a) residential projects costing $1,000 or more and not involving more than four residential units; and, (b) commercial projects costing $1,000 or more, but less than $60,000 must provide the owner with a "Notice to Customer". This notice identifies the contractor and relates registration and bonding information. The form must be signed by the customer and retained for three (3) years. Failure to provide this notice voids any lien rights that a contractor dealing directly with the owner would otherwise have. This notice is required by the contractor registration statutes (18.27 et. seq.) and should not be confused with the notices given under the lien statutes. Failure to give this notice is also a violation of the Washington State Consumer Protection Act (19.86 et. Seq.).

SEE FORM B

   B.   NOTICE TO OWNER OF RIGHT TO CLAIM A LIEN (RCW 60.04.031)

   Who Must Give Notice: The notice to owner is required to be given by certain persons furnishing professional services, materials, or equipment for the improvement of real property. It may also be called a "materialmen's" or "preclaim" notice. Failure to give this notice voids lien rights, someone would otherwise have, for providing professional services, materials or equipment.

1. Professionals, Suppliers and Lower Tier Subcontractors

   Professionals, material and equipment suppliers who do not have a contract directly with the owner, and second tier or lower tier subcontractors must provide a "NOTICE TO OWNER"

   a) Form of Notice: The statutory form must be used.

   b) Timing of Notice: The notice must be provided within 60 days of the first work or material delivery on a commercial project; 10 days for new construction of single family projects. After that time, a lien can only be claimed for work, equipment or material delivered within the 60 or 10-day period put prior to the notice being provided.

   c) Delivery of Notice: The notice must be sent to the owner and the general contractor. The notice must be mailed, return receipt requested, or personally served with a signed acknowledgement of receipt. The lien claimant need not prove that the notice was actually received. (BAKER v. ALTMAYER 70 Wn. App. 188, 851 P.2d 1257, 1993)

Those individuals contracting directly with the general contractor are not required to provide the notice. However, it is still a recommended procedure.

SEE FORM C

2. <u>Owner-Occupied Single Family Residential Remodels</u>:
   Those contracting directly with the general contractor (except for laborers) must give the <u>Notice to Owner</u>, to owners occupying residences to be remodeled.
   a. <u>Generally</u>: Those who contract directly with the owner/occupier of an existing single-family residence for its remodel, repair or alteration do not need to send the notice to owner of right to claim a lien and their right to claim a lien is not restricted.
   b. <u>Exceptions</u>: Except laborers, everyone not contracting directly with the owner/occupier must give the notice to owner. Those providing professional services or materials must provide the notice.

SEE FORM C

3. <u>Providers of Professional Services</u>
   a. <u>Generally</u>: In order to provide notice to possible lenders or buyers, professionals must <u>record</u> a new and separate notice in the real property records of the county where property is located when they provide

"preconstruction activities". Such activities are preparing plans, specifications, surveys or other engineering services. This notice is record prior to the beginning of the actual construction.

b. Recording of Notice: All professionals must record a notice with the County Auditor stating the professional's name, address, telephone number, legal description, owner or reputed owner's name and general nature of professional services. No time frame is set in the statute for this recording. Absent actual or constructive notice, the failure to file subordinates the lien as to subsequent lenders and invalidates the lien as to subsequent purchasers.

c. Contents: This notice must contain:
   1. The provider's name, address and telephone number;
   2. The legal description of the property;
   3. The owner or reputed owner's name; and
   4. A general description of the services provided.
   5. A legal description is mandatory in this notice.

SEE FORM D

d. Exceptions: This notice need not be recorded:
   1. When the services are "visible" from inspection of the property;

2. When persons dealing with the property have actual notice the services were provided; or
3. Once actual construction starts, then notice of the services is presumed.

   e. <u>Consequences</u>: Failure to record the notice as discussed previously would invalidate the lien as to the interests of a bona fide purchaser and subordinate the lien to the interest of a lender, but <u>will not</u> affect the lien rights as against the original owner.

III. <u>FILING THE LIEN</u>

A. <u>CREATING THE LIEN (RCW 60.04.091)</u>

1. <u>Lien Filing Requirements</u>: The lien attaches to improvements and to the property as of the date the first work (labor or material) was done on the site. The Claim of Lien must be recorded with the county auditor where the property is located within 90 days from the last day labor, equipment, material or professional services were supplied to the property.

The Lien must be served or mailed by certified or registered mail to the owner <u>within 14 days of recording</u>. Failure to do so will <u>preclude an award of attorney fees and costs to the claimant</u>.

2. <u>Contents of Claim of Lien</u>:
   a) The name, address and phone number of the claimant;

b) The first date labor or materials was furnished;
c) The last date labor or material was furnished;
d) The name of the person in contract with the claimant;
e) The name of the owner or the person reputed to be the owner, if not known, state not known. The lien is valid against community property, even if the claim of lien names only one spouse. The better practice however is to name both spouses.
f) The street address or other description of the property reasonably sufficient for identification. (If at all possible, the property should be described by a complete legal description. See discussion in B.1. below).
g) The principal amount for which the lien is claimed.
h) A lien may be assigned, and if assigned, the name of the assignee must be stated in the claim of lien.
i) A sample <u>Claim of Lien</u> is contained in the statute.

SEE FORM E

B. <u>RECORDING REQUIREMENT (RCW 65.04.045)</u>
   1. <u>County Auditor's Recorded Instrument Requirements</u>:
      a) First page must contain:

- three-inch margins at top and bottom;
- one-inch margins bottom and each side;
- return address upper left corner;
- document title;
- reference numbers of documents assigned or released;
- grantor;
- grantee;
- legal description;
- Assessor's property tax parcel account numbers

2. Failure to comply will cause lien to be rejected and will cause delay and possible loss of lien rights.

SEE FORM F

C. <u>AVAILABILITY OF INFORMATION (RCW 60.04.230 and 261)</u>
   1. <u>Generally</u>: On construction projects exceeding $5,000, the general contractor is required to post a notice in plain view on the job site listing the owner's name, address and phone number; the legal description or tax parcel number; registration number, the general contractor's name, address and phone number; and the name, address and phone number of the lender or payment bond issuer.
   Failure to post the notice is a misdemeanor.

2. The contractor is to provide information to suppliers and subcontractors when their identity becomes known.

D. THE AMOUNT OF THE LIEN (RCW 60.04.091)

1. Generally: The lien is for the unpaid contract amount, or the reasonable value if there is no written contract. While recoverable, the lien claimant should not include interest, fees or costs in the amount claimed in the Claim of Lien.

2. Owner-Occupied Residential Remodels: Lien claims of this sort are limited to the general contract amount which the owner has not paid to the general contractor when the Notice to Owner was served on the owner (RCW 60.04.031). This limitation does not apply to labor claims.

IV. FORECLOSING THE LIEN

A. LAWSUIT MUST BE FILED WITHIN 8 MONTHS (RCW 60.04.141)

Once a claim of lien has been filed, legal action, in the Superior Court in the County where the property is located, to enforce the lien must be commenced within eight months after the recording date of the Claim of Lien; otherwise the lien expires. Attorney's fees and costs are awarded to the prevailing party, in an amount determined by the court.

B. BOND IN LIEU OF CLAIM (RCW 60.04.161):

Generally: The owner may record a surety bond, in an amount equal to the greater of five thousand dollars or two times the amount of the lien claimed if it is ten thousand dollars or less, and in an amount equal to or greater than one and one-half times the amount of the lien if it is in excess of ten thousand dollars. The lien then attaches only to the bond. The same rules regarding foreclosure apply to the bond proceeds.

C. THE "STOP PAYMENT" NOTICE TO THE LENDER (RCW 60.04.221):

1. Generally: The "Stop Payment" notice does not require the lender to pay the claimant. The "Stop Payment" procedure is not available if a payment bond of at least 50% of the construction financing has been posted by the general contractor or owner. The potential claimant must maintain its right to a mechanic's/materialman's lien and properly file the notice to "Real Property Lender" ("stop notice").

2. Procedure: A lien claimant who has not received payment within five days after the date required by the contract, may, within 35 days after payment is due, give the lender the notice "Real Property Lender". The notice must be sent to the lender administering the construction loan, with copies to the owner and the general contractor. The notice should be sent registered or certified mail, return receipt requested.

3. <u>The Effect of the Notice to the Real Property Lender</u>: Failure of the lender to withhold from the loan disbursements the amount stated in the notice causes that amount to be given priority over the lender's security.

SEE FORM H

D. <u>THE OWNER'S RIGHTS AGAINST A LIEN CLAIMANT (RCW 60.04.81</u>:
   1. <u>Procedure</u>: The owner or general contractor may challenge a Claim of Lien or notice to Real Property Lender. The statute provides for an expedited court proceeding. It must be shown that the lien is "frivolous, made without reasonable cause or clearly excessive". The prevailing party may be awarded attorney's fees and costs.
E. <u>LIEN RELEASE (RCW 60.04.071)</u>:
   1. A lien must be released "immediately" upon payment.

SEE FORMS I, J and K

V. <u>CONSUMER PROTECTION</u>

A. <u>VIOLATION (RCW 60.04.035)</u> The statute has a provision regarding consumer protection violations. <u>Acts of coercion</u> or attempted coercion, including threats to withhold future contracts, by a contractor or developer <u>to discourage</u> someone from giving a notice of right to claim a lien or from filing a claim of lien is a violation of the Consumer Protection Act (RCW 19.86 et seq.) and an unfair or deceptive act or practice in trade or commerce.

B. PENALTY (RCW 19.86 et seq.): As a consumer protection violation, the claimant would be entitled to normal damages, plus attorney fees and treble damages as a penalty up to a maximum of $10,000. The statute provides that requiring potential lien claimants to waive lien rights by contract may be a violation; to threaten the loss of future contracts or future jobs in order to obtain that lien waiver would be a violation.

VI.   PRIORITY OF LIENS—WASHINGTON STATE

A. LIEN PRIORITIES (RCW 60.04.181)
   1. Liens for performance of labor
   2. Liens for contributions owed to employee benefits plan
   3. Liens for furnishing material, supplies or equipment
   4. Lien for subcontractor, including but not limited to their labor and materials
   5. Lien for prime contractor or for professional services
B. The proceeds from the sale of any property sold in a lien foreclosure action is applied first to pay liens in a class before any is applied to pay the next lower class. When there are not enough proceeds to pay an entire class in full, then the proceeds are applied pro rata to that class.
C. Liens are subordinate to deeds of trust or mortgage which attached or were recorded

prior to " . . . the time of commencement of labor or professional services or first delivery of materials or equipment by the lien claimant" (RCW 60.04.061).

LIEN SUMMARY

Office Procedure Form

Type: Washington   Job No. _____
                  Private Work   P.O. No. _____

Owner's Residence or Place of Business	Jobsite	General Contractor or Agent	Architect

☐	Notice to Customer Commence	Send <u>Notice to Customer</u> (Form B) immediately when your customer is the owner.
☐	Notice to Owner	Send <u>Notice to Owner</u> (Form C) to the owner and general contractor by certified mail return receipt requested within 1-10 days for new <u>single family</u>, or 1-60 days for <u>commercial buildings</u>, after the first delivery date or commencement of services.

A) First Delivery Date or Commencement of Services_____
B) Commercial (60 days) [ ] Single Family (10 days) [ ]
C) Preliminary Notice Date _____Nos. _____
D) First Invoice No. _____and due date _____
E) Notice to Lender can be sent 5 days after invoice due and no more than 35 days. Use Form H.

☐	Final Notice and Lien	Record final notice (Forms E and F) within 1-90 days after last delivery or performance with County Auditor where project is located (or request attorney to do so).

A) Last Delivery Date or Performance Date_____

B) Final Notice and Lien Date _____No._____

C) Legal Description Secured_____

D) Last Invoice No._____

E) County Auditor Recording Date_____County_____

_____

FORM A

☐ Commence Foreclosure Action — Notify attorney to commence foreclosure action within 8 months after recording final notice with County Auditor. Allow sufficient time for attorney to prepare foreclosure action (recommended no later than 90 days prior to expiration of 8 months).

A) Notification of Attorney Date _____
B) Send Copies to Attorney
   1) Lien Summary
   2) Contract and Invoices
   3) Payment Ledger Schedule
   4) Preliminary Notice and evidence of mailing and receipt
   5) Final Notice and Lien with evidence of mailing
   6) Additional Charges
   7) Legal Description of Property

FORM A-2

NOTICE TO CUSTOMER

This contractor is registered with the state of Washington, registration no._____, and has posted with the state a bond or deposit of _____for the purpose of satisfying claims against the contractor for breach of contract including negligent or improper work in the conduct of the contractor's business. The expiration date of this contractor's registration is _____.

THIS BOND OR DEPOSIT MIGHT NOT BE SUFFICIENT TO COVER A CLAIM THAT MIGHT ARISE FROM THE WORK DONE UNDER YOUR CONTRACT.

This bond or deposit is not for your exclusive use because it covers all work performed by this contractor. The bond or deposit is intended to pay valid claims up to that you and other customers, suppliers, subcontractors, or taxing authorities may have.

FOR GREATER PROTECTION YOU MAY WITHHOLD A PERCENTAGE OF YOUR CONTRACT.

You may withhold a contractually defined percentage of your construction contract as retainage for a stated period of time to provide protection to you and help insure that your project will be completed as required by your contract.

YOUR PROPERTY MAY BE LIENED.

If a supplier of materials used in your construction project or an employee or subcontractor of your contractor or subcontractors is not paid, your property may be liened to force payment and you could pay twice for the same work.

FOR ADDITIONAL PROTECTION, YOU MAY REQUEST THE CONTRACTOR TO PROVIDE YOU WITH ORIGINAL "LIEN RELEASE" DOCUMENTS FROM EACH SUPPLIER OR SUBCONTRACTOR ON YOUR PROJECT.

The contractor is required to provide you with further information about lien release documents if you request it. General information is also available from the state Department of Labor and Industries.

I have received a copy of this disclosure statement.

_____

(signature of customer)

FORM B

NOTICE TO OWNER

IMPORTANT: READ BOTH SIDES OF THIS NOTICE CAREFULLY.

PROTECT YOURSELF FROM PAYING TWICE

To: _____

Date: _____

Re: _____ (description of property: Street address or general location.) _____

From: _____

AT THE REQUEST OF: _____ (Name of person ordering the professional services, materials, or equipment. _____

THIS IS NOT A LIEN: This notice is sent to you to tell you who is providing professional services, materials, or equipment for the improvement of your property and to advise you of the rights of these persons and your responsibilities. Also take note that laborers on your project may claim a lien without sending you a notice.

OWNER/OCCUPIER OF EXISTING RESIDENTIAL PROPERTY

Under Washington law, those who furnish labor, professional services, materials, or equipment for the repair, remodel, or alteration of your owner-occupied principal residence and who are not paid, have a right to enforce their claim for payment against your property. This claim is known as a construction lien.

The law limits the amount that a lien claimant can claim against your property. Claims may only be made against that portion of the contract price you have not yet paid to your prime contractor as of the time this notice was given to you or three days after this notice was mailed to you. Review the back of this notice for more information and ways to avoid lien claims.

COMMERCIAL AND/OR NEW RESIDENTIAL PROPERTY

We have or will be providing professional services, materials, or equipment for the improvement of your commercial or new residential project. In the event you or your contractor fail to pay us, we may file a lien against your property. A lien may be claimed for all professional services, materials, or equipment furnished after a date that is sixty days before this notice was given to you or mailed to you, unless the improvement to your property is the construction of a new single-family residence, then ten days before this notice was given to you or mailed to you.

FORM C

Sender: _____

Address: _____

Telephone:_____

Brief description of professional services, materials, or equipment provided or to be provided:

_____

_____

_____

IMPORTANT INFORMATION FOR
YOUR PROTECTION

This notice is sent to inform you that we have or will provide professional services, materials, or equipment for the improvement of your property. We expect to be paid by the person who ordered our services, but if we are not paid, we have the right to enforce our claim by filing a construction lien against your property.

LEARN more about the lien laws and the meaning of this notice by discussing them with your contractor, suppliers, Department of Labor and Industries, the firm sending you this Notice, your lender, or your attorney.

COMMON METHODS TO AVOID CONSTRUCTION LIENS: There are several methods available to protect your property from construction liens. The following are two of the more commonly used methods.

DUAL PAYCHECKS (Joint Checks): When paying your contractor for services or materials, you may make checks payable jointly to the contractor and the firms furnishing you this notice.

LIEN RELEASES: You may require your contractor to provide lien releases signed by all the suppliers and subcontractors from whom you have received this notice. If they cannot obtain lien releases because you have not paid them, you may use the dual payee check method to protect yourself.

YOU SHOULD TAKE APPROPRIATE STEPS TO PROTECT YOUR PROPERTY FROM LIENS.

YOUR PRIME CONTRACTOR AND YOUR CONSTRUCTION LENDER ARE REQUIRED BY LAW TO GIVE YOU WRITTEN INFORMATION ABOUT LIEN CLAIMS. IF YOU HAVE NOT RECEIVED IT, ASK THEM FOR IT.
cc: Prime Contractor   Certified Mail #_____
                              Return Receipt Requested____

FORM C-2

NOTICE OF FURNISHING
PROFESSIONAL SERVICES

That on the *(day)* day of *(month and year)*, *(name of provider)* began providing professional services upon or for the improvement of real property legally described as follows:

[Legal description is mandatory]

The general nature of the professional services provided is _____

_____

The owner or reputed owner of the real property is _____

_____

_____

_____(Signature)_____

_____(Name of Claimant)_____

_____(Street address)_____

_____(City, state, zip code)_____

_____(Phone number)_____

cc: Owner (if appropriate)   Certified mail #
Return receipt
requested

cc: Prime Contractor   Certified mail #
                                   Return receipt
                                   requested
 cc: Claimant's Customer   Certified mail #
(If other than owner Return receipt requested or Prime
Contractor)

FORM D

After recording return to:

_____[claimant]

_____

_____[address]

CLAIM OF LIEN

_____, Claimant vs.

_____(name of person indebted to claimant)_____

Notice is hereby given that the person named below claims a lien pursuant to chapter 60.04 RCW. In support of this lien the following information is submitted:

1. <u>NAME OF LIEN CLAIMANT:</u>
   <u>TELEPHONE NUMBER:</u>
   <u>ADDRESS:</u>

2. <u>DATE ON WHICH THE CLAIMANT BEGAN TO PERFORM LABOR, PROVIDE PROFESSIONAL SERVICES, SUPPLY MATERIAL OR EQUIPMENT OR DATE ON WHICH EMPLOYEE BENEFIT CONTRIBUTIONS BECAME DUE:</u>

_____

_____

3. <u>NAME OF PERSON INDEBTED TO THE CLAIMANT:</u>

_____

4. DESCRIPTION OF THE PROPERTY AGAINST WHICH A LIEN IS CLAIMED (street address, legal description or other information that will reasonably describe the property):

_____

5. NAME OF THE OWNER OR REPUTED OWNER (If not known state "unknown"):

6. THE LAST DATE ON WHICH LABOR WAS PERFORMED; PROFESSIONAL SERVICES WERE FURNISHED; CONTRIBUTIONS TO AN EMPLOYEE BENEFIT PLAN WERE DUE: OR MATERIAL, OR EQUIPMENT WAS FURNISHED:

_____

7. PRINCIPAL AMOUNT FOR WHICH THE LIEN IS CLAIMED: _____

_____

8. IF THE CLAIMANT IS THE ASSIGNEE OF THIS CLAIM SO STATE HERE: _____

_____

_____, Claimant

_____
(Phone number, address, city and state of claimant)

FORM E

STATE OF WASHINGTON   )
) SS.

COUNTY OF   )

_____, being sworn, says: I am the claimant (or attorney of the claimant, or administrator, representative, or agent of the trustees of an employee benefit plan) above-named; I have read or heard the foregoing claim, read and know the contents thereof, and believe the same to be true and correct and that the claim of lien is not frivolous and is made with reasonable cause, and is not clearly excessive under penalty of perjury.

_____

I certify that I know or have satisfactory evidence that __ _____is the person who appeared before me, and said person acknowledged that signed this instrument and acknowledged it to be _____free and voluntary act for the uses and purposes mentioned in the instrument.

Dated: _____.

_____
NOTARY PUBLIC in and for the State of Washington, residing at
My Commission expires:

cc: Owner   Certified mail #
                               Return receipt requested
 cc: Prime Contractor   Certified mail #
                               Return receipt requested
 cc: Claimant's Customer Certified mail #
(if other than owner Return receipt requested or prime contractor)

FORM E-2

COUNTY AUDITOR INDEXING COVER SHEET

WHEN RECORDED RETURN TO:

Name: _____

Address: _____

City, State, Zip:_____

DOCUMENT TITLE(s)

1. _____
2. _____
3. _____
4. _____

REFERENCE NUMBER(s) OF DOCUMENTS ASSIGNED OR RELEASED:

☐ Additional numbers on page of document

GRANTOR(s):

1. _____
2. _____
3. _____

☐ Additional names on page of document

GRANTEE(s):

1. _____
2. _____
3. _____

☐ Additional names on page of document

LEGAL DESCRIPTION

Lot-Unit: ___Block: ___Volume: _____Page:____

Section: ___Township: _____Range: ____

Plat Name:_____

☐ additional legal description is on page of document

ASSESSOR'S PROPERTY TAX PARCEL ACCOUNT NUMBER(s):

☐ additional legal description is on page of document

The Recorder will rely on the information provided on the form. The staff will not read the document to verify the accuracy or completeness of the indexing information provided herein.

FORM F

THE CONSTRUCTION SITE POSTING REQUIREMENT
Washington State Mechanics' & Materialmen's Liens

PROPERTY OWNER _____

ADDRESS _____

TELEPHONE _____

JOB SITE ADDRESS _____

LEGAL DESCRIPTION OR TAX PARCEL # _____

CONTRACTOR _____

ADDRESS _____

TELEPHONE _____

REGISTRATION NO. _____

LENDER AND/OR BONDING COMPANY _____

ADDRESS _____

TELEPHONE _____

FORM G

NOTICE TO REAL PROPERTY LENDER

(Authorized by RCW 60.04.221)

TO: _____ (Name of Lender) Certified mail # _____
_____ Return Receipt Requested _____

_____ (Administrative Office—Street Address) _____

_____ (City, State, Zip) _____

AND TO: _____ (Owner) Certified mail # _____
Return Receipt Requested _____

AND TO: _____ (Prime Contractor—if Different than
Owner)
_____ Certified mail # _____
_____ Return Receipt Requested _____

_____ (Name of Laborer, Professional, Materials or
Equipment Supplier) _____
whose business address is: _____
did at the property located at _____
(check appropriate box) _____
□ perform labor
□ furnish professional services
□ provide materials
□ supply equipment as follows: _____

_____

which was ordered by _____(Name of person)_____
whose address was stated to be _____
_____

    The amount owing to the undersigned according to contract or purchase order for labor, supplies or equipment (as above mentioned) is the sum of _____
_____Dollars ($_____). Said sums became due and owing as of _____

    You are hereby required to withhold from any future draws on existing construction financing which has been made on the subject property (to the extent there remain undisbursed funds) the sum of _____
Dollars ($_____).

FORM H

IMPORTANT

Failure to comply with the requirements of this notice may subject the lender to a whole or partial compromise of any priority lien interest it may have pursuant to RCW 60.04.226 of this act.

DATE: _____

By: _____

Its: _____

cc: Claimant's Customer
(If other than owner or
Prime Contractor)

Certified mail #_____
Return Receipt
Requested

FORM H-2

_____
Claimant

RELEASE OF LIEN

_____
Defendant

KNOW ALL PERSONS BY THESE PRESENTS, that a certain Lien, claimed by Lien Notice filed and recorded in the office of the County Auditor of _____County, Washington, on the _____day of _____ _____, 20_____, recorded under Recording No. ___ _____, by the above-named claimant against the above-named defendant, for the sum of _____ Dollars ($ _____) upon the following property:

_____
_____
_____

is paid and satisfied, and the same is hereby released.

_____
Claimant

_____
[address]

FORM I

STATE OF WASHINGTON   )
) ss.
COUNTY OF   )

    I, _____, being sworn, says:

    I am the claimant above-named; I have read or heard the foregoing Release of Lien, read and know the contents thereof, and believe the same to be true and correct.

_____

                Claimant

    GIVEN UNDER MY HAND AND OFFICIAL SEAL this ____
_____ day of _____, 20 ___ .

        NOTARY PUBLIC in and for the State
        of Washington, residing at _____
        My Commission expires: _____

FORM I-2

_____

Claimant

PARTIAL RELEASE OF LIEN

_____

Defendant

KNOW ALL PERSONS BY THESE PRESENTS, that a certain Lien, claimed by Lien Notice filed and recorded in the office of the County Auditor of _____ County, Washington, on the _____ day of _____, 20____, recorded under Recording No. _____, by the above-named claimant against the above-named defendant, for the sum of _____ Dollars ($_____) upon the following property:

has been partially paid and is partially satisfied in the amount of $_____, and the same is hereby partially released in said amount.

_____

Claimant

_____

[address]

FORM J

STATE OF WASHINGTON   )

) ss.

COUNTY OF   )

I, _____, being sworn, says:

I am the claimant above-named; I have read or heard the foregoing Release of Lien, read and know the contents thereof, and believe the same to be true and correct.

_____

Claimant

GIVEN UNDER MY HAND AND OFFICIAL SEAL this ____ _____day _____of _____, 20___.

NOTARY PUBLIC in and for the State of Washington, residing at_____
My Commission expires: _____

FORM J-2

_____

Claimant

CONDITIONAL RELEASE OF LIEN

_____

Defendant

KNOW ALL PERSONS BY THESE PRESENTS, that a certain Lien, claimed by Lien Notice filed and recorded in the office of the County Auditor _____ of County, Washington, on the day _____ of _____, 20____, recorded under Recording No. _____, by the above-named claimant against the above-named defendant, for the sum of _____ Dollars ($_____) upon the following property:

is hereby paid and satisfied, and the same is hereby released, conditioned upon the check in the amount of $_____ issued by _____ clearing the bank.

_____

Claimant

_____

[address]

FORM K

STATE OF WASHINGTON   )
) ss.
COUNTY OF   )

I, _____, being sworn, says:

I am the claimant above-named; I have read or heard the foregoing Release of Lien, read and know the contents thereof, and believe the same to be true and correct.

_____
Claimant

GIVEN UNDER MY HAND AND OFFICIAL SEAL this ____
_____ day of _____, 20___.

NOTARY PUBLIC in and for the State
of Washington, residing at
My Commission expires: _____

131

INDEX TO
WASHINGTON STATE PUBLIC WORKS BOND
CLAIMS
(RCW 39.08 et seq.)

INDEX TO
WASHINGTON PUBLIC WORKS RETAINAGE CLAIMS
(RCW 60.28 et seq.)

FORMS

CLAIM SUMMARY

PRECLAIM NOTICE TO CONTRACTOR BY
SUBCONTRACTOR'S
MATERIALMAN OR SUPPLIER

NOTICE OF CLAIM OF LIEN OF MATERIALMAN OR
SUBCONTRACTOR AGAINST BOND OF CONTRACTOR ON
PUBLIC WORK AND AGAINST
TRUST FUND RESERVED BY PUBLIC BODY

WASHINGTON STATE PUBLIC WORKS BOND CLAIMS

(RCW 39.08 et seq.)
SEE FORM A

I.   BOND OR 50% RETAINAGE IN LIEU OF BOND

    A. BOND REQUIRED (RCW 39.08.010):
      1. Any contract for a public improvement by Washington State, or any county, municipality or other public body within Washington, requires a surety bond in the amount of 100% of the contract amount except:

        a) When the contract is for thirty-five thousand dollars or less' then at the option of the contractor, the public body may retain 50% of the contract price for a period of 30 days after the date of final acceptance, or until receipt of all necessary releases;

        b) When the contract is for $100,000 or less, an individual surety or sureties may be substituted for a surety company.

    B. FAILURE TO OBTAIN BOND (RCW 39.08.015):
      1. In the event the public body fails to obtain a bond from the contractor or follow one of the two exceptions above, the public body becomes liable to the full extent and for the full amount of all debts contracted for by the contractor. This does not include the State.

C. PARTIES PROTECTED (RCW 39.08.010):
   1. The bond protects all:
      a) Laborers;
      b) Mechanics;
      c) Subcontractors;
      d) Materialmen;
      e) All persons who supply the contractor or subcontractors with provisions and supplies for the furtherance of the contract.
D. NOTICE TO CONTRACTOR (RCW 39.08.065):
   1. When materials are furnished to someone other than the general contractor, the person providing those materials must give notice to the contractor no later than 10 days after the first delivery.
   2. Substantially, the notice shall contain the following:
      a) That the claimant has commenced to deliver materials, supplies or provisions;
      b) The name of the subcontractor or agent ordering them;
      c) That the contractor and the bond will be held liable for payment;
      d) That a claim against the bond may be made.

SEE FORM B

E. NOTICE TO PUBLIC BODY (RCW 39.08.030):
   1. The person claiming against the bond must file a notice of the claim with the public body

no later than <u>30 days</u> after acceptance of the project by the public body.
2. Contents of the claim (RCW 39.08.030):
   a) The name of person or firm filing the claim;
   b) The amount of the claim;
   c) The name of the general contractor and the bonding company;
   d) The description of the public contract; and
   e) The signature of the claimant or authorized agent.

SEE FORM C

3. The claim must be provided to:
   a) Contractor;
   b) Bonding company;
   c) Public body; and
   d) Party with whom claimant is doing business.
4. Notice may be given by registered mail return receipt or personal service and obtaining a receipt.
F. <u>FORECLOSURE AGAINST THE SURETY BOND</u> (RCW 39.08.030):
   1. The lawsuit for foreclosure of the bond is commenced in the Superior Court. Attorney's fees shall be awarded to the claimant in an amount the Court determines reasonable. The exception is that no attorneys fees may be allowed if the lawsuit for foreclosure is

commenced less than 30 days after the date of filing the notice with the public body.

2. The lawsuit for foreclosure must be brought no later than 6 years after filing the notice with the public body, or the time limit contained within the bond itself.

3. Interest may be allowed at the statutory rate commencing from the date the claim is filed, with the public body.

G. PRIORITY OF CLAIMS

1. The bond statute does not establish any priority for payment of claims. This would generally not be an issue because the bond is for the full contract price of the project.

WASHINGTON PUBLIC WORKS RETAINAGE CLAIMS

(RCW 60.28 et seq.)
SEE FORM A

I.   <u>RETAINED TRUST FUND</u>

A. <u>RETAINAGE REQUIRED (RCW 60.28.010)</u>: Any "public body"; contracting for public improvements and/or work on public facilities are required to reserve from the money earned by the contractor a sum not exceeding 5%. This amount is to be withheld from each progress payment.

B. <u>PARTIES PROTECTED (RCW 60.28.010)</u>:

1. The retention is a Trust Fund for the protection and payment of any person or persons, mechanic, subcontractor, or materialperson who performs labor or provides materials for a public improvement contract, and any other person who supplies the person with provisions or supplies for the carrying on of a public improvement contract. Persons, include partnerships and corporations, who:

    a) <u>Perform labor</u>, or
    b) <u>Furnishing supplies toward completion of public improvements</u>.

2. If monies are withheld, at the option of the contractor the funds retained shall be:

a) Retained in a fund by the public body;
b) Deposited by the public body in an <u>interest bearing account in a financial institution</u>, interest is payable to the contractor;
c) Placed in escrow with a bank or trust company. The deposit will be invested in bonds and securities chosen by the contractor and approved by the public body with interest payable to the contractor.

3. With consent of the public body, the contractor may provide a bond (which is in addition to the bond required by RCW 39.08 et seq. discussed earlier) and not have retainage withheld.

4. Retained funds must be paid to the contractor within sixty (60) days of completion of all contract work on the public improvements. The payment is subject to the provisions of RCW 39.12 et seq. and RCW 60.28 et seq.

C. <u>NOTICE TO GENERAL CONTRACTOR (RCW 60.28.015)</u>:
1. When materials or equipment are furnished to anyone <u>other</u> than the general contractor, notice must be given to the general contractor in writing by:
    a) Mailing by return receipt, registered or certified mail in an envelope addressed to the contractor, or
    b) By serving the notice personally upon the contractor or the contractor's representative and obtaining a receipt;
2. Materials covered by notice:

c) The notice is effective for materials or equipment, furnished during the 60 day time period preceding the giving of the notice and all subsequent materials or equipment.

3. The notice must state:
    a) That the claimant has furnished materials and/or equipment;
    b) The name of the subcontractor ordering the materials and/or equipment; and
    c) A lien against the retained percentage may be claimed for all materials and/or equipment furnished.

SEE FORM "B"

D. NOTICE TO PUBLIC BODY (RCW 60.28.011):
1. Notice of claim against the retained funds must be given to the public body.
2. The notice of claim:
    a) Must be filed with the board, council, commission trustees or officer acting for the public body at any time after the account balance is due but no later than 45 days after completion of the contract work;
3. The notice of claim to public body must contain (RCW 39.08.030):
    a) The name of person or firm filing the claim;
    b) The amount of the claim;
    c) The name of the general contractor and the bonding company;

d) The description of the public contract; and
   e) The signature of the claimant or authorized agent.

SEE FORM "C"

4. The notice of claim must be provided to:
   a) General contractor;
   b) Bonding company;
   c) Public body; and
   d) Party with whom claimant is doing business.
   e) Notice may be given by registered mail return receipt or personal service and obtaining a receipt.

E. FORECLOSURE OF LIEN AGAINST THE RETAINED FUND (RCW 60.28.030):
   1. Any claim against the retained fund may be foreclosed against the retained fund by commencing a lawsuit in the superior court in the county where the claim was filed within four months of the date of giving notice of the claim. A prevailing claimant is entitled to recover reasonable attorney's fees as determined by the court, and interest from the time of filing the notice of claim.

F. PRIORITIES (RCW 60.28.040):
The retained fund is disbursed according to the following priorities:
   1. Wage claims under prevailing wage statutes;
   2. All taxes and penalties owed to the State of Washington arising out of the contract;

3. All other claims for labor, materials supplies or equipment;
4. All other taxes and penalties;
5. In the event there is not enough monies to pay the claims in any category the claimants in that category share on a pro rata bases, in the available funds.

CLAIM SUMMARY

Office Procedure Form

Type: Washington   Job No. _____
                Public Work   P.O. No. _____

Public Body: Name and Address	Jobsite	General Contractor or Agent	Architect

☐   Preliminary Notice* Send Claim Notice (Form B) by registered or certified mail, return receipt requested, no later than 10 days for claims against the bond and within 60 days for claims against the retainage after first delivery date to General Contractor.

A) First Delivery Date _____
B) Preliminary Notice Date _____ Nos. _____
C) First Invoice No. _____

☐ Notice of Claim*   Send Notice of Claim
                          (Form C) by registered
                          or certified mail, return
                          receipt   requested,
                          no later than 30 days
                          after   acceptance   of
                          the PUBLIC BODY IN
                          CHARGE with a copy to
                          the General Contractor
                          and surety for claims
                          against the bond and 45
                          days after completion
                          for claims against the
                          retainage.

A) Last Delivery Date or Performance Date _____
B) Final Completion and Acceptance Date _____
C) Notice of Claim Date _____No. _____

---

*As a practical matter, Forms B and C may be used as a claim against both the bond and retainage and can be filed once.

FORM A

☐ Commence
Foreclosure Action

Notify attorney to commence foreclosure action within 30-120 days after filing notice.

A) Notification of Attorney Date
B) Send Copies to Attorney
    1) Claim Summary
    2) Contract and Invoices
    3) Payment Ledger Schedule
    4) Preliminary Notice and evidence of mailing and receipt
    5) Notice of Claim with evidence of mailing
    6) Additional Charges

FORM A-2

PRECLAIM NOTICE TO CONTRACTOR BY SUBCONTRACTOR'S MATERIALMAN OR SUPPLIER

TO: <u>(Name and address of Contractor)</u>

You are hereby notified that the undersigned claimant has furnished ____<u>(materials, supplies, or equipment)</u>____ for use in the prosecution of the work of _____ , at the request of_____. The first day of delivery was _____. If the undersigned is not paid for these materials, it will file a claim against you and retainage held by the _____ for payment of any sum that is due and owing to the undersigned.

You are further informed that your bond will be held for payment of any sum that is due and owing to the undersigned.

  DATED this _____day of _____, 20___.

    Name of Claimant _____

    Address _____

    Phone Number _____

    _____

    Signature

    Title _____

    Contractor Registration Number _____

cc: Claimant's Customer   Certified mail # _____
                                        Return receipt
                                        requested

        Surety   Certified mail #
                                        Return receipt
                                        requested

FORM B

NOTICE OF CLAIM OF LIEN OF MATERIALMAN OR SUBCONTRACTOR AGAINST BOND OF CONTRACTOR ON PUBLIC WORK AND AGAINST TRUST FUND RESERVED BY PUBLIC BODY

CERTIFIED MAIL
RETURN RECEIPT REQUESTED

TO: [Name of state, county, municipality or other public body]

NOTICE IS HEREBY GIVEN that the undersigned, _____

_____, has a claim in the sum of $_____ and against the bond taken from _____ (name of principal) _____, principal, and _____ (surety on the bond) _____, for the work _____

_____ (brief description of the work for which the bond was taken with address of the place of construction and work done by claimant _____

NOTICE IS FURTHER GIVEN that the undersigned has a claim for said sum against the sum retained by said Public Body as a trust fund for the protection and payment of the undersigned, pursuant to RCW 60.28.010.

DATED this _____ day of _____, 20___.

[Company] _____

[Address] _____

By: _____

cc: Prime Contractor   Certified mail #
                                         Return Receipt Requested
cc: Surety Certified mail #
                                         Return Receipt Requested
cc: Claimant's Customer Certified mail #
                                       Return Receipt Requested

BOND CLAIM
OUTLINE AND PROCEDURES
FEDERAL PUBLIC WORKS

Copyright James H. Hopkins 2011

INDEX TO

BOND CLAIMS ON FEDERAL PUBLIC WORKS PROJECTS—"THE MILLER ACT" (40 USC § 3131

SEE FORM A

I. <u>WHEN A BOND IS REQUIRED (40 USC § 3131)</u>

    A. Contracts for construction, alteration or repair of any federal public project, require the prime contractor to furnish a payment bond, although the contracting body shall provide alternatives to payment bonds for protection of suppliers of labor and materials under contracts that are more than $25,000 and not more than $100,000.

    B. The amount of the bond required is equal to the contract amount, unless the contracting officer determines such an amount impractical; in which case the amount shall be set by the contracting officer.

II. <u>PARTIES PROTECTED BY THE BOND (40 USC § 3131)</u>

    A. Persons or firms involved in work on a federal construction project who have a direct contractual relationship with either:
      1. The prime contractor; or
      2. Subcontractors, who have a direct contractual relationship with the prime contractor.

III. <u>NOTICE REQUIREMENTS (40 USC § 3131)</u>

    A. Every subcontractor, supplier or laborer who does not have a direct contractual relationship with the prime contractor must give written notice to the prime contractor within 90 days of the last day of furnishing labor or materials.

B. Inspection of work completed, nor correction of defective work extends this time period.

C. The notice must provide with substantial accuracy:

   1. The amount claimed; and

   2. The name of the subcontractor to whom the labor or material was furnished.

SEE FORM B

The notice must be provided to the contractor in such a manner as to provide third-party verification of delivery, i.e. by registered or certified mail with return receipt requested, Federal Express™, or personal service through a third party.

IV. FORECLOSURE OF CLAIM AGAINST BOND (40 USC § 3131)

A. A foreclosure action against a Miller Act bond surety must be commenced in federal court in the federal district where the work took place.

B. The foreclosure action must be commenced within one year from the date of last furnishing labor or materials.

C. Interest on the claim may be allowed from the date payment is due.

D. There is no provision for attorney's fees under the Miller Act.

E. When the contract between the parties allows for recovery of attorney's fees, a court may grant them as part of the monies owed.

F. When the claims exceed the face amount of the bond, the claimants will share pro rata.

CLAIM SUMMARY

Office Procedure Form

Type: Federal   Job No. _____

              Public Work   P.O. No. _____

Public Body: Name and Address	Jobsite	General Contractor or Agent	Architect

☒ Preliminary Notice   No Preliminary Notice necessary.

A) First Delivery Date _____
B) Preliminary Notice Date: <u>None</u> Nos. <u>None</u>
C) First Invoice No. _____

☐ Notice of Claim   Send Notice of Claim (Form B) by registered mail, return receipt requested, no later than 90 days after last delivery or performance to the General Contractor or Agent with copies to the Bonding Company and owner.

A) Last Delivery Date or Performance Date _____

B) Final Notice and Lien Date _____ No. _____

C) First Invoice No. _____

D) Last Invoice No. _____

E) Bonding Co. Name _____

Address _____ District _____

FORM A

☐ Start Suit   Notify attorney to start suit within one year after last delivery or performance.

A) Notification of Attorney Date _____
B) Send Copies to Attorney
    1) Lien Summary
    2) Contract and Invoices
    3) Payment Ledger Schedule
    4) Preliminary Notice—None
    5) Final Notice and Lien with evidence of mailing
    6) District Marshal Record—Not Necessary
    7) Additional Charges

FORM A-2

MILLER ACT NOTICE TO CONTRACTOR

TO: _____ (prime contractor) _____

You are hereby notified that the undersigned claimant has furnished (labor, materials, supplies or equipment) for use in the prosecution of the work of (public agency, contract number) at the request of (name of subcontractor). The last day of furnishing (labor, materials, supplies or equipment) was _____.
The undersigned makes claim against you and your surety for payment of $_____ which sum is due and owing to the undersigned.

DATED this _____ day of _____, 20____.

Name of Claimant _____
Address _____
Phone Number _____

_____
Signature
Title _____
Contractor Registration Number _____